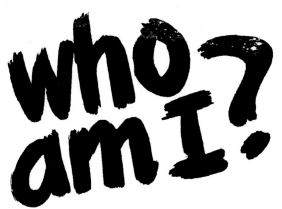

who am I?

women talking and writing
about their lives

First published in 1982 by The Gatehouse Project
Reprinted 1986 and 1995 by Gatehouse Books Ltd.

Text copyright © Individual authors 1982

Editors, Patricia Duffin and Stella Fitzpatrick
Cover design, David Andrassy
Photographs page 1 Patricia Duffin; page 10 split Image; page 18
Manchester Studies; pages 6, 34 The Guardian; pages 20, 22
Manchester Libraries; pages 30, 32 Gatehouse Project; page 16 Buzz Logan
Illustration page 26 Fanny Tribble
Back cover poem, Janet Taylor

Published and distributed by Gatehouse Books Ltd.
Hulme Adult Education Centre, Hulme Walk, Manchester M15 5FQ

Typesetting: Roe Cross Graphics
Printing: L.V. Lawlor, Oldham

ISBN 0 90625313 6
British Library cataloguing in publication data:
A catalogue record for this book is available from the British Library

Gatehouse is grateful to the Equal Opportunities Commission (EOC)
for the grant which allowed the writing group to meet and covered
initial production costs.

Gatehouse gratefully acknowledges continued financial support from
Manchester City Council and North West Arts Board

Gatehouse is a member of the Federation of Worker Writers and
Community Publishers (FWWCP)

CONTENTS

WHO ARE WE?

We want to use these pages to tell you about ourselves and how we ended up here in print.

For many of us, coming to the Monday night group was more of a night-out to start with, not so much wanting to write but wanting to be involved in something, a challenge. We came because we already knew other women in the group. It took time for us to get easier with one another; we'd be just warming-up when it was time to go home! Now we wish more women could get together as we do, to talk and write about how they feel about their lives.

We've discovered a lot about ourselves, as well as being surprised to find ourselves writing. We each had our own difficulties about spelling and grammar when we joined the group, but slowly realized that worrying about these made us lose the ideas we were trying to get onto paper. So now we put it all down, and worry about the look of it afterwards. We also found that the more we wrote the better we felt about it. Part of each meeting we spend writing; then we stop for tea and a chat, then read what we've written (or taped) to the rest of the group. A lot of times you underestimate yourself. You think, "Well, I don't think that's very good," and then some-one else will say "Well, I like that." It helps to hear what the others think.

When we started to talk about what would go into this book we set aside time every other week to read through the writing and talk about it. At first, we found it very difficult to say No to anything, because we knew how much work had gone into each piece. However, as the weeks went by it got easier to see what we all liked and wanted to share with you. Some of the writing came from women who had written in other Gatehouse groups. Some pieces we asked to be made clearer, or felt we'd like to see with a different title, and we talked with the writers about this.

We were very lucky to have the support of the Equal Opportunities Commission (EOC) throughout all this, so there was money for bus fares and a creche. They also covered our expenses for a weekend in the Lake District to do the final work on this book, as well as paying the printing costs. This photograph and the poem on the back cover came out of this weekend, as well as all the decisions about photographs, drawings and the idea of dividing the book up into sections. Also this introduction.

As soon as the book comes back from the printers we plan to have a reading party to launch it, with all our family and friends who've come to accept that Monday is our night, to spend as we choose.

Many things have happened to us since we first met to write, our weekend together being one of the most exciting. Some of us have read and talked to literacy students from all over the north-west at a 'Write First Time' writing weekend; others at the national get-together of the Federation of Worker-Writers and Community Publishers, to which Gatehouse belongs. We play to go on meeting to write and talk, and read to each other. We hope some of you will join us in your part of the country. We'd like to hear from you if you do.

APRIL 1982

Josie Anderson   Stella Fitzpatrick

Janet Taylor.   Julie Matthews

Pauline Murphy.   Patricia Duffin

e. A. Connor.

Leah Hood   Stella Ford.

Doreen Rawlinson

3

Who Cares?

DOWNTRODDEN FEMALE

Why do all men think that they are superior? Why is it that you always hear men saying: "It's a woman's job, you should do that". After all, what is a woman's job? Come to that, what's a man's job?
A coalminer, well we could do that too.
A carpenter.
A surgeon.
A lorry driver.
A car mechanic.
A steel worker.
An electrician.
A bricklayer.
Many a woman could do this.

The only difference between us and them is that we carry the babies. This only proves that we are the stronger. Men are like babies especially when they're ill. Us women just plod on regardless.

Most men are slags and sluts. They have to sleep around with as many different women as they can just to prove they are a man. Woman is always a woman, she never has to prove herself. I think it's time the tables were turned. Stick the pinnies on all these ninnies, give them a mop and a broom and the shopping list and the toilet brush and the pan scourer and the dirty nappies and the dirty sheets and the ironing and the washing and the baby to nurse and then ask him why is he tired and fed-up. "You've been at home all day with nothing to do but play games with the baby."

Diane

5

THE MENOPAUSE

Will it ever end?
This no-man's land
That every woman has to tread
Alone and in despair
What lies ahead . . . ?

THE BOMB

Rotting flesh
Wide-eyed and grotesque
Not much longer before oblivion.

Doreen Ravenscroft

7

NEARLY RAPED

This stands out clearly in my mind. I don't think I've ever felt so sick before. I knew the boy. Jimmy, that was his name. I knew his mum very well. She had the greengrocers over the road.

I'd gone to Carriages, a night club in Droylsden, and he was there. Quite good looking, I remember thinking to myself. He came over to the bar where I was standing with my friend. He said Hello, and then offered to buy me a drink. I accepted. I remember feeling quite good at the time because I liked him and he was a good looking boy. We stayed together for the rest of the night, chatting about all sorts. I didn't think he fancied me, he just knew me.

He offered me a lift home, he only lived over the road from me. We walked to the car which had been parked behind the club. He got in the back, I couldn't understand why. I asked him before I got in, "Why are you in the back?"
He said, "Oh it's not my car, it's Brian's. He'll be here in a minute." I believed him, so I sat beside him. That's when it started. Pushing me down, mauling me. I was confused and wondered why, what's happening? He started pulling at my clothing, first my blouse, then my skirt. I fought with him, pleading and crying.
"Don't bring on the tears," he said, "That won't get you anywhere."
He was very strong, no match for me. My heart was thumping. I could hear it in my ears. Then I wanted to be sick, I felt cheap and degraded, the scum of the earth. He almost had me till I bit his cheek. I ran from the car. Sobbing. Sick. Dirty and bedraggled.

Diane

VANDALISM

VANDALISM
WHY? Frustration. Hearts sad because
Kids are pitched way up high,
In the sky.
Don't make noise,
Parents lose their poise.
Anger, unhappiness reigns.
Lower the music,
Turn down the radio,
Turn off these noisy plays
Get out of the block.
The caretaker will come
He'll report to the Council,
The Housing Lady will come.
Quieten your kids.
Or you'll be put on the defaulters list.

Two more complaints
Eviction

Mrs. Joan McGee

BED OF THORNS

What is marriage? It is a bed of roses? More like a bed of thorns. To me it has felt like I have been stuck on a thorn bush unable to get off or out. Nothing but arguments, broken pots, smashed windows. Occasionally I would get the odd black eye, more often than not I got kicked or thumped where no-one would see. I have even had milk bottles thrown down the street at me. Why do men do this? If I only knew. After eleven years I still don't know. When I was 8½ months pregnant I was thrown top to bottom of the stairs. I still remember the drop. Only to find out a week later when my daughter was born she had a dislocated hip due to my trip. I even got a broken nose the day my daughter was christened.

I've tried to understand why men stoop so low to behave this way. Is it a weakness? From my experience I find things go bump when the mood takes. He is really like a bear with a sore arse when he comes home from work. He has his tea then goes to sleep for a couple of hours. More often than not when he wakes up he is in a favourable mood, spruces himself up ready for a few jars. As if that solves it. Not by a long way. I can get anything from being thrown out of the house, dragged out of bed or even locked out of the bedroom. I have often thought where the saying 'You made your bed, you lie in it' came from. Well, I found out alright but there's only so many thorns your body will take.

Zad

LIFE SO FAR

Life so far has been a pain
A constant solitary confinement
Lost virginity at 13
An abortion at 16
21 I'd had a kid
26 I'd had another
I might mention not of the same colour
People call me a whore
Shout "Bastards" at my kids
To hell with your condemnations
I've no regrets
Except perhaps two
Life so far has been hell
Yet another cock up
Screwed every white son-of-a-bitch
Wearing jeans
Even fancied a teacher once
I get a kick out of speed
Drink till I'm pissed
Valiums are my breakfast
Brandy is my lunch
End pressures with a sleeping pill
Authority impounded my kids
Crucified me thoroughly
Now, I'm well and truly a whore.

Ronke

SEAL SONG

I often think how life was before
We were hunted, our skin torn.
I lived in peace upon the sea
Till man came to murder me.
They took my coat so pure and white
And didn't give me a chance to fight.
What right have men to take my coat from me
Then disappear back into the sea?

I often think what life was before
Men came to kill us by the score.
To take from us our coats so white
And leave us raw upon the ice.
Can fashion-conscious women see
What wearing my coat has done to me?

Janet Taylor

As
Time
Passes

OLD AGE

Old age can be such a trial.
Stiff bones, getting out of a chair,
Going upstairs, just walking.
Everything an effort.
Pain, loneliness, suffering,
Depending on other people.

Old age can be such a joy.
A job well done, a loving family,
Grandchildren.
Peace to enjoy what you want to do,
When you want to do it.
Contentment.

Josie Anderson

MY MOTHER

My mother is ninety one years of age. She can still walk about and she can still read a book, she doesn't have a walking stick. My mother likes good food. She always said, "Good food and plenty of rest to keep you going." My mother liked the old days when they went to work on an open bus. How the years have changed and the people have changed. In them days people would help one another. There wasn't the violence in them days like there is today. At one time, round town used to be all fields, then the money people come along and started to build cotton mills and factories.

About three years ago I gave work up to look after my mother. The doctor told me she needed somebody to be with her all the time. I was told to go to the Social Security. They asked me for a doctor's note, I didn't have one. They said get a doctor's note and send it to them, then I would get a visitor and they would help me. But when I got a visitor he was very nasty. He told me I would not get anything at all as my name was not on the rentbook. I don't think it was fair at all. I have always worked and the first time I wanted a little bit of help I was turned down. But if you were to tell a lot of lies, then you can draw the benefit. If they are encouraging people to tell a lot of lies, if they think some people are slow and can't read and write, they take liberties.
If people can't get things in an honest way then they will lie.

Leah Hood

MY BATH NIGHT

Every Friday evening about five thirty I take myself to the public wash baths in Herbert Street for my weekly bath. I have done this since I was ten years old, it is part of my way of life.

In those days I went to the wash baths with my sister. You paid two old pennies and were allowed a half an hour and eight inches of water. An attendant would take you to a cubicle in which there was a bath, stool, a mirror on the wall and also a mat on which to stand after you come out of the bath. The attendant would draw the water for you, and there were taps with a special key and once the water was drawn that was all you were allowed. So you bathed quickly before the water went cold.

A lot of people used these wash baths in the thirties, forties and fifties, before houses were made with a bathroom. The wash baths today are different. Not many people go and so you have more time to yourself. They also have taps which turn on and off and you can run as much hot water as you like. The fee for this and a nice clean towel is twenty pence. I stay for my bath for one hour and a half. I find this a great pleasure and if they ever were to close these wash baths I would be very upset indeed.

Doreen Ravenscroft

MAY THE FIRST

When I was in work yesterday I overheard someone ask the date, and a man answered, "May the first". I'd forgotten it myself and in a surprised voice I said, "O yes, it is. Has anyone seen any horses dressed up?" But nobody had of course because these days every day's the same. You don't know if it's Christmas or Easter, as my mother used to say.

It got me thinking of May Days when I was young. What great times we had. My friend Alma and I always had a maypole. We always like to sew. We'd save a couple of pennies up and buy some coloured paper and make aprons and capes for the girls, sashes and headbands for the boys. Then we'd look for a pole off some old brush and cover that with paper in different colours and tie lengths of string round the top. Next we'd have to get a round piece of wood, we called a garf. The next article was the most difficult – a long piece of lace curtain. The only curtains around were the ones up at the windows, but we always seemed to get one in the end. That was for the Queen's train, the Queen being some pretty little girl about five or six. We'd tie the curtain round her neck then have two girls holding the ends of it. We'd get the boys, brothers and their friends for dancing round the pole – the biggest boy had to hold it in the middle while the others held a piece of string each. Alma and I, being the bosses, held the garf which we held in front of the Queen's face. In her hands she carried a box or tin for the money.

Then after a lot of trouble (mostly from the boys who didn't want to dance, we were off from door to door singing our little song hoping to get a penny or ha'penny. As soon as we'd get

about threepence we'd run and get some more different colours of paper to make more clothes, so we'd have the best maypole. Then we'd start again from door to door, trying to get the most money so we could beat some other group. So it went on until we were fed up. Then we would all gather in our back yard for the great event of sharing out the money which was maybe a penny or twopence each – to us the best part of a good day.

Josie Anderson

APRIL

I feel sad that once such a brilliant yellow
is now withered brown petals.
Your body bent after such a strong straight show.
One of my favourite sights is to see you in
your thousands scattered under the trees.
Golden heads on lovely green bodies
against the black earth.
Yet you seem to stay such a short time
after being so long awaited through the
cold dark winter.
Thank God you will appear next year
like an old friend
a never ending pleasure.

Josie Anderson

Laugh
With
Us

BOTTOMS UP

One night my friends and I went out to town for a night out. There was about six of us. We went to Oscars for a drink first. It was crowded but we found a table and got the drinks. We was having a really good time. After about an hour I went to the toilets with one of my friends. We had to talk right across the room, it was at the other end. That night I was wearing a black maxi skirt as they were the fashion at the time. When I came out of the toilet and was putting some make-up on at the mirror, I noticed some girls giggling but I didn't think anything about it. My friend was behind me as we came out and she let me walk all the way back to the table with the hem of my skirt tucked into the top of my knickers, showing all my bottom. When we got to our table she was nearly in hysterics. I was so embarrassed, I could have died. I got my coat and bag and got out as quick as I could. When the other girls came out, all falling all over laughing, I had to laugh myself.

We went on to this club and this so-called friend who had let me walk through the pub walked straight to the bar, fell off her platform shoes and pulled a bowl of crisps all over herself. She looked ridiculous on the floor with crisps all over her hair, but to my mind, justice was done.

Coleen Connor

NEVER SAY DYE

It was last Saturday. I bought a red chiffon blouse last week. I'd fallen madly in love with it as soon as I'd seen it. What I didn't realise at the time I tried it on was that you could see through it. By the time Saturday came, the night I was going to wear it, I had to start dashing about for a red bra. I tried lots of shops around my area, but to my dismay was unsuccessful. I sat at home pondering what could I do? "I will wear this blouse."

Then I had a great idea. "I'll get a dye and dye one of my old bras red." Off I went again. Sadly, the haberdashery was shut. So I went home again. By this time I'd given up.
I sat and thought, "What can I do?" and then the silliest idea came into my head, "I'll dye it with a food dye." I did this with essence of raspberry. It worked, it was great. I had my red bra.

After arguing with my boyfriend over how ridiculous it was and how I would stink of raspberries, I threw it in the bin.
"I'll buy a red bra this weekend."

Diane

Taking
A
Chance

THE CLEANER

Well, that's me. I think cleaning is one of the worst jobs there is, even though I do it myself. I think people that do cleaning jobs are housewives, they do part-time cleaning because the hours suit them. Now there's the people like me who do this job because they can't do anything else. My writing and spelling isn't very good so I can't fill in forms or go in for any other sort of job. I am doing a cleaning job now five until eight. There are only four of us there including me and I've got the job as supervisor, only because I know about cleaning not because I am outspoken or anything, and it doesn't make me feel good being supervisor of a cleaning job. I would rather it be of something else.

Well I drag myself there every night, go in, take my coat off and collect my cleaning tackle. The place is quite big so I sectioned the offices off between the other girls, making sure no one had any more than anyone else, because you find that causes a lot of trouble between them. I don't do offices. I've got the job all cleaners don't like – that's toilets. The office staff always look down on us. I think they think we're people from another planet with no brains. It's a job that has to be done by someone, but they make it hard for us by throwing the litter around the bins instead of in them, and spill their tea all over the corridors, the ones I have to buff every night. Well I am determined to do something about all this. I have started a course at North Hulme College brushing up on my maths and English. Well, maybe one day it will be the other way round, like me sitting behind a desk making a mess instead of cleaning it.

Linda Davies

29

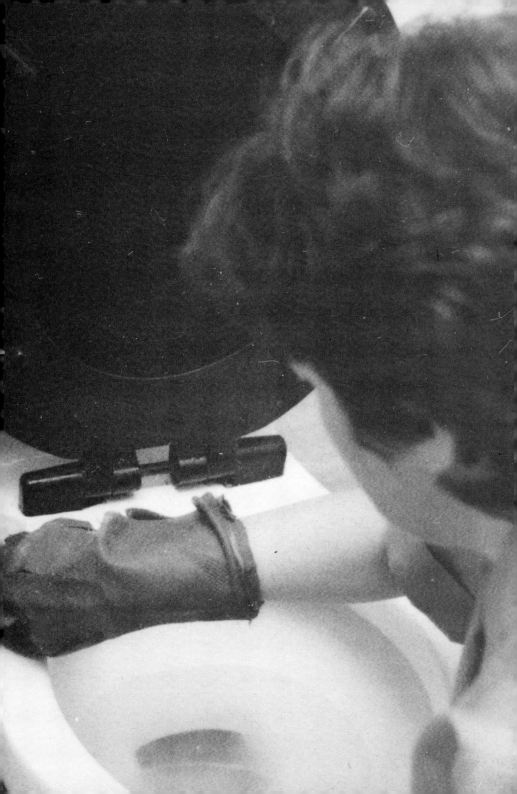

NEVER TOO LATE

The thing I regret most in my life is that I did not apply to join the T.S.D.* course sooner. I am forty six years old and for the first time in my life I am really happy in what I am doing.

I was born before the last war in 1935. My school days were not really happy because I was always worried an air raid was going to start; also I had my little sister to look after and had all sorts of jobs to do at home.

When I left school I became a machinist because the only thing I was good at was using my hands, or so my mother told me. I got married and had my family which consists of two boys, so my time was spent bringing them up.

Now I have some time to spend on myself I feel I am doing the right thing.

Pauline Murphy

A government funded course to improve job prospects.

SEEING THE LIGHT

I remember when I first left school, that's when it hit me. I realized there wasn't much choice in jobs for me because I didn't pay much attention at school. I remember feeling really sick about wasting my school days. I really loved school, I thought it was one big laugh. I was in the bottom class at school so the teachers didn't have much time for us. The English teacher used to give us a pack of cards or dominoes to play with and the maths teacher was that young he was too busy weighing the girls up. So as you know I didn't get much done. I wasn't really bothered at the time because I was having such a good time. I used to say to my friends, "You won't catch me in a factory machining all day."

Well where do you think I ended up? In a factory, machining. It was my first job. I quite enjoyed it at first because there was a lot of young girls starting like me so we used to have a laugh. Anyway after a couple of years it wasn't such a laugh any more, it became very boring. The same thing day in day out. I would get up in the morning, be in work for 8 o'clock and it was still dark at that time. Then we would finish at 5 o'clock and then it would be dark again so I was never seeing daylight only at weekends or if I had a day off and I couldn't afford that because of the wages. I was only getting £5 a week, that was in 1970 though, but it was still low. I used to sit at that same machine all day looking at the clock most of the time and that made it drag more.

Anyway, one day I was just thinking to myself, "What the hell am I doing sat here like a robot, just something to work these horrible machines?" Anyway the sun was shining outside so I

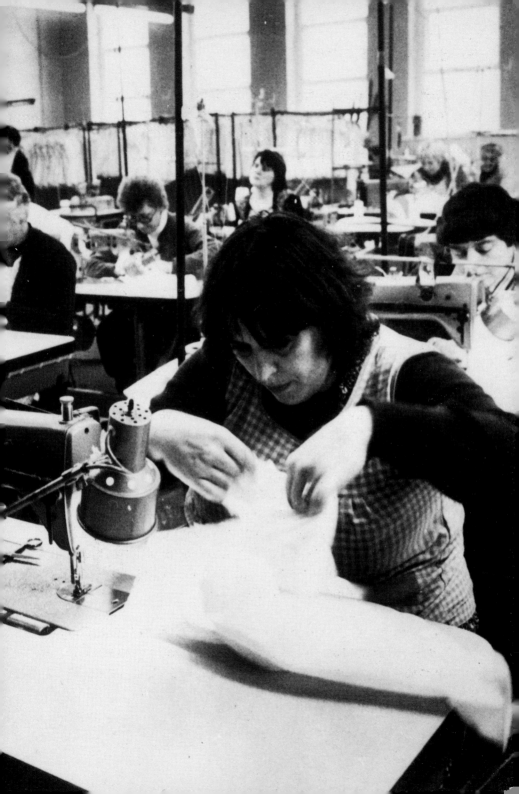

thought, a young girl like me should be out enjoying it while you can. So up I got, went to the boss and handed in my notice. His face looked shocked, he tried to talk me out of it, not because he was sorry to lose a good machinist because he couldn't be bothered finding someone else. Well off I went running up the road feeling very free. It was great. I ran round to my friend who was out of work at the time. So we had a talk and decided to go working down south in a hotel doing chambermaid. I know it's still work but it's a much nicer place and atmosphere down there plus you get lots of fresh air, and a nice tan, and that's more like it to me. So I went and spent all summer there, it did me the world of good, that break.

Linda Davies

Gatehouse Books

Gatehouse is a unique publisher

Our writers are adults who are developing their basic
reading and writing skills. Their ideas and experiences
make fascinating material for any reader, but are particularly
relevant for adults working on their reading and writing
skills. The writing strikes a chord – a shared experience of
struggling against many odds.

The format of our books is clear and uncluttered. The
language is familiar and the text is often line-broken, so that
each line ends at a natural pause.

Gatehouse books are both popular and respected within
adult basic education throughout the English speaking
world. They are also a valuable resource within secondary
schools, special needs education, social services and within
the prison education service and probation services.

Booklist Available

Gatehouse Books
Hulme Adult Education Centre
Hulme Walk
Manchester M15 5FQ
Tel: 0161 226 7152

The Gatehouse Publishing Charity is a registered charity reg. no. 1011042. Gatehouse Books Ltd is a
company limited by guarantee, reg. no. 2619614.